26 Things to Teach your Parents

by Marlena Jareaux

INSPIRED
—BY THE—
BEACH
PUBLISHING

There are several people that I would like to thank who helped me with this book by providing their valuable comments and suggestions: my mother (Martha Brice), Dr. Lanning Moldauer, Linda Friskey, LCSW-C, Dr. Tanya Greenfield, Sylvia Pearson and my son Kaleb. I am grateful to each of them for their time, patience and support.

I would also like to thank the many people with whom I have interacted with in the past, for without them, I would not have had the inclination to seek the guidance and inspiration that helped me to get where I am today. While there are too many to name here, I would be remiss if I didn't mention my mentor Sylvia Pearson who has provided me with years of support, love and wisdom, the Reverend Sylvia Sumter of Unity of Washington, DC who has provided me and so many others with invaluable life lessons (like "your thoughts are prayers")that are oh so useful and "on time" ("and that's the truth!"), my uncle Theodore Holmes who showed me at an early age the value of consistently pursuing your dreams, my best friend Kim Stokes (my twin, confidant and sounding board that helps me to "keep it real"), my son who reminds me daily that despite my age I still have a lot to learn, and my mother who from day one believed I was worth fighting for and continues to be my biggest fan!

Designed by Jennifer Arbaiza Graphic Design

Illustrated by Rusty Haller

Page design and typesetting by JustYourType.biz

Printed in the United States of America

LCCN: 2006938735

ISBN: 978-0-9790415-1-8

able of Contents

Why You Should Read This Book...

Message for tweens/teenagers:

Being you isn't easy, is it? Being a person between the ages of 10 and 14 isn't easy. I'm sure that you already know this by now. It can seem like no one understands you. You may be thinking that your parents don't know anything about what it is like being a kid your age, or that times were very different when they were a child. It is true that the world is a much different place than it was when your parents were young. But it is also true that the path your parents had to take when they were kids is essentially the same path that you are getting ready to take...you just don't know it yet. Your parents thought that their parents (your grandparents) didn't know what they were talking about. They also thought that their parents didn't remember what it was like being a kid. Just to set the record straight, the same little boy or girl that used to be your parents when they were younger, is still somewhere inside your mom and dad. A couple of things have changed though. Mortgage or rent payments, jobs, bills to pay, food to buy and make, diapers for your little brother, lunch money for you....the list goes on and on. All of these things that have to be taken care of by your parents makes it sometimes impossible for the little girl or little boy inside them to come out and play. Doesn't mean that they don't want to, just that there never seems to be enough hours in the day for them to BOTH work AND play.

You may think that you don't yet have a place here in this world. There is a cartoon on Cartoon Network that many of you have probably seen before. It's called Codename: Kids Next Door. In case you've never seen the show, it is about five 10-year olds who have one mission in life: to save kids all over the planet from the unfair rule of adults. Many of you have probably watched or heard of this show and wondered to yourself "Yeah, why is it that adults have to rule the world...why can't kids rule the world?" I won't bore you with charts, graphs and speeches on why you can't rule the world. What I will tell you is that your place right now is not to rule the world (maybe you'll rule a company or our country later though). You are growing, learning and living so that one day, you will be an adult who has responsibilities....but who lives, loves and hopefully leaves this world in better condition than it was when you came into it. I hope that this book answers some questions for you and helps you to find your way (and your place) in this world. The future of us adults depends on YOU.

Message for parents/guardians/adults:

This book was written with your children and their parents in mind (YOU), and your parents, for that matter. One of the ideas that is covered in this book is "If you want something different, then do something different." Keeping that thought in mind, this book is my gift to children and you parents that do so much for them (regardless of their age). It is my hope that any person of any age who picks up this book and reads it will at least learn one thing that can help them through their life. The world has become quite different than the days of my childhood in York, PA. Gone are the days of leaving your front door unlocked, and watching your child leave the house in the morning and having them not return until the streetlights begin to flicker on (and not having any idea where they've been all day or who they've been with). My mother has always told me that she does not envy my having to raise a child (and a boy at that) in these days and times. People always say that kids are so resilient and can get through almost anything. Though my son Kaleb is only 10 years old at the time of this writing, there isn't a day that goes by that I don't realize that my actions and decisions today will forever affect his life and times tomorrow. I, like you, want the best for my child, and want him to grow up to be the confident, successful and happy man that I've seen in his eyes ever since I first looked into them on the day he graced my life with his appearance in it. Fortunately, he has people in his life that equally share concerns about his future abilities to fare well in a society and world that is so different from that in which we were raised. I'm sure your son/daughter has similar people. Someone who wants him to be able to handle the streets and the people that can sometimes be so mean, unfair and at times somewhat vindictive. Others, who do their best to make sure that your child has some exposure to and gets some spiritual defenses from a church, synagogue or other institution. And still others (like teachers and caretakers) who work hard each day to show your child love and compassion while trying to educate them about the ever-changing and challenging world that lies ahead for them.

How do you raise a child in these days and times? You arm them with as much knowledge, love and opportunities that you possibly can. The rest, as they say, will be up to your child's willpower, desires, and the hand of God (or whatever you believe your Higher Power to be). I didn't have a book like this when I was growing up. I've read many inspiring and helpful books as an adult, but when my own son started asking me questions and became conscious of the start of the many complexities and situations of life, I realized that I had to try to condense what I've learned as an adult into useful packets of information that could help him. Hoping that I'd find something written that would eliminate him saying, "Oh mom, you don't know everything" or "Oh, how long is this speech going to take", I searched in Border's and at Amazon.com to no avail. I found wonderful books and titles for teenagers, but nothing short and sweet enough to hold the attention of my 10 year old. I hope that this book fits the bill for my son, for your child, and for you. Maybe you will pickup one or two new ideas in the process that you will find to be helpful for you. Enjoy!

P.S. I always enjoy hearing from people. If you'd like to comment on anything that I have written, offer suggestions for things you'd like to see included in book 2, just email me at mjareaux@hotmail.com.

26 Things to Teach your Parents

You can never take it back.

People say words to each other every day.

What's for dinner?

Thank you.

Can I help clean up?

Can we have pizza for dinner?

I love you Mom.

Sometimes the words that you say are funny. Sometimes, you say things to people that you want them to know. And sometimes you tell people how you feel with your words. You may think they're just words... after all, they're just combinations of the ABCs right?

When you say words to people, you have to be careful about your choice of words. Words can make a person feel good, but they can also make them feel bad. For example, if you are angry with someone, you might decide to tell them how you are feeling. An example:

Tina and Betty are playing a game together. Tina has more points than Betty.

Tina: "I love playing this game. I'm really good at it."

Betty: "You're only good at it because you cheat."

Tina: "I don't cheat!"

Betty: "Yes you do. You're a cheater."

Tina: "No I'm not! I'm just good at it. Now, I want you to leave."

Betty: "I was just kidding."

If you were Tina, how would you feel about what Betty said? How would you feel if someone called you a cheater? How about if someone called you a liar? Betty was upset because Tina had more points than her and she thought that she was losing, but she should not have called Tina a cheater just because she was frustrated at the thought of possibly losing.

Remember the saying "sticks and stones may break my bones but words can never hurt me"? Well, that's not 100% true. The truth is, words can sometimes hurt you much more and for a longer time than a punch in the stomach. Once the words leave your mouth and are said to someone else, you can never really 100% take them back. You can try to apologize for saying them, and the person may say that they forgive you. However, even though they may forgive you, it doesn't mean they will forget. Choose carefully the words that come out of your mouth. Think before you speak.

There was a young girl who loved to sing every chance that she got. Everyone told her that she had a beautiful voice. It made her feel good to sing, and she thought she was good at it. One day, her mother had a rough day at work, and she came home frustrated. The girl started singing like she always did, but her mother was so upset about her day, that she yelled at the girl and told her to "stop that awful noise." The girl stopped singing – permanently. Be careful of what you say…it can't be taken back.

2.

Say what you mean and mean what you say.

If someone asks you how you feel about something, it is important to say what you really mean. Find the "right" way and time to tell the person how you feel. Don't try to throw them off the trail by telling them half-truths about what you feel. Try not to beat them over the head with how you feel.

If your parent asks you why you did something, don't tell them what YOU THINK THAT THEY WANT TO HEAR. If they ask you why you failed your end-of-unit test, don't tell them that the teacher didn't go over any of the materials and that's the reason you weren't prepared. If you think that reason is a good one to tell because it shows that it's not your fault (and you probably won't get grounded if it's not your fault), think again. If your parent decides to call your teacher to ask them why they gave you a test in math on things that you've never learned, or if they ask your teacher at parent-teacher conferences, the truth is going to come out. Then, you will likely have not only your parents upset with you (and not trusting you because of a lack of integrity), but also your teacher who will be wondering what she did to deserve having you lie about her. Does it sound worth it to take that chance of having so many people not trust you?

Let's think of it in another way. Let's say that you want your parent to play a board game with you. You ask if they will be able to play one with you tonight after dinner. They say "sure I can...right after dinner". You are eating your cheeseburger, and are even managing to get through the green beans quickly because you are so excited about playing with your parent. Once you're finished, you rinse off your plate, put it into the dishwasher, clear the table (your household chore) and run upstairs to get a selection of board games to bring downstairs. You dash down the steps barely able to keep your balance on the steps because you are holding 5 board games. You run into the living room and place them all in a circle on the floor. At this point, it doesn't matter to you which game is played...you like them all...and you just really want to play with your parent. You look around you and start to wonder why your parent isn't on the floor with you. After about 10 seconds, you call out their name. There is no answer. You get up, walk into the kitchen and still can't find your mom/dad. You still call their name, while walking up the steps. When you get to the top of the stairs, you see (much to your horror), that your mom/dad is sitting at their desk in front of the computer. You can't hide your disappointment as you ask "what about our game, are you coming"? Your parent says "Oh, honey, I just have to check my email and pay some bills online. Give me about 10 minutes." Ten minutes later, your parent says they need another twenty, and twenty minutes later, they say that they didn't mean that they were going to play a board game TONIGHT. If this is the third time this week that this happened, will you think that your parents "say what they mean and mean what they say?"

Make sure that you say what YOU mean, and mean what YOU say.

3.

Do your best, but realize that your best changes every day.

If you try to play a game of sports, how you do in the game will depend on how prepared you are. If you eat a healthy breakfast, you'll be more prepared to play well in your game. If you didn't get much sleep the night before, didn't eat breakfast, and had an argument with your brother the morning of the game, then you may not play as well as you have played in the past.

We start each day with a certain energy level. Almost everything that you do can either add to or subtract from that energy level. Eating healthy can add to your energy, while having just a donut for breakfast can take away from it. Getting enough sleep can help you to feel refreshed and restored the next day. If you don't get enough sleep, you may be easily frustrated, you will likely get tired more quickly, and you may not be able to pay attention for long.

Therefore, your best changes everyday. What your best is on Saturday can be very different than what your best is on Sunday. Don't feel bad if your best is different today than it was yesterday. That is going to happen. Try not to compare today's best to last week's best. Give yourself permission (tell yourself that it's okay) to have days where your best is not as good as it's been before. Tomorrow is another day.

Don't take things personally.

Sometimes when people say things to you, the things that they say don't really have anything to do with you. Ever been able to tell when someone was in a bad mood? A friend or a family member may have had a bad day at work or school, they came home or near you, and then you asked them a simple question like "Do you want to play some of my cool video games"? Your friend says "They're not so great. I know people who have better games than you", or your family member says "You know, they're just video games. Speaking of which, you don't take care of them as well as you should. I spent a lot of money on them. You must think that money grows on trees."

Feeling confused? Wondering what happened? Wondering what you did wrong? You may feel confused, and you may wonder what happened, and though it's easy to wonder if you did anything wrong by asking if your friend or family member thinks you have cool video games, try not to. Let's look at this a little closer:

Friend: "They're not so great. I know people who have better games than you."

There could be many reasons why this friend doesn't share your feelings about your video games. Maybe they really don't like the games you have. Maybe they are a little jealous that you have a game that they don't have. Or maybe they were just punished by their parents and aren't allowed to play with their own games, so they don't want to talk about your games.

Family member: "You know, they're just video games. And you don't take care of them as well as you should. I spent a lot of money on them. You must think that money grows on trees."

Can you think of any reasons why this family member started talking about video games but then ended up basically saying that money doesn't grow on trees?

Your parents aren't going to tell you everything that is going on in their lives. Their job is to raise you the best they can (remember about doing your best?) so that one day you'll be able to take over that job. Protecting you from harm, as well as providing you with food, clothing, shelter and an education is also their responsibility. There are many decisions that have to be made each day of your parents' lives, and many things that happen to your parents each and every day. Some of those things you will see and witness, and some of them you will never hear or know about. Perhaps the family member in the above example just had to pay a large bill and is now worried about where they're going to get the money for something else. Maybe the raise in their paycheck amount that they thought they were going to get never happened. These are just some of the reasons why someone may be sensitive to money issues. The point is, just because someone says something to you, doesn't mean that it has anything at all to do with you. Sometimes, what someone says to you, or how they say it to you, has to do with themselves or how they are feeling about something.

Don't take it personally.

5.

Don't make assumptions.

The definition of "assumption" is "a statement accepted as true without proof"(The American Heritage Dictionary, 1983, p. 42) … that's right, I had to look in a dictionary to be able to give you this definition, and it won't kill you to open up one every now and then so that you can be clear on what a word means...I've had this one for the past 20 years and I still use it.

You may think that you know for sure the reasons why someone has done or said something. There may appear to be one and only one reason why you think that your friend said what they said or did what they did to you today. In the following examples, the first part is what happened, and the part in parentheses is what you think the reason was for it being done or said:

Zach said that he hates me (because he really does).

Courtney kicked my soccer ball over the fence (because she doesn't want to see me have fun).

Ethan didn't come over to my table at lunchtime (because he doesn't want to be my friend anymore).

If you believe your first thought about the reasons why the people in your life do what they do, you may be making a big mistake. Sometimes, what you think and how you act is caused by how you feel. Let's look at an example:

You go to school and are surprised by a pop quiz from your math teacher. You weren't 100% ready for the test, so you are a little nervous about how you did on the test. You won't know what grade you received until tomorrow. When you get home from school, your friend Brendan comes over to play. After he's played with you for 5 minutes, he says that he is bored and wants to go home. He says he will see you another day, and he goes home. When your mom asks you where your friend is, you almost burst into tears and tell your mom that Brendan left because he doesn't like playing with you. Brendan didn't actually say anything at all about not liking you or not liking to play with you. It's a good chance that you are much more sensitive to things because you are unsure of your abilities as a result of the surprise test.

Unless you are 100% sure of the EXACT reason why someone in your life has done or said something, don't assume that the reason is the first one that is coming into your head or thoughts. Instead, give it some more thought, and ask questions in order to be sure. If you react to an incorrect assumption, you may have more of a mess to clean up later.

6.

Let your actions match your intentions (what you mean to do).

Words are easy to say. They are easy to have slip out of your mouth, but as we've discussed, aren't easy to take back once they've been said. Sometimes, words are the best things to use in order to let someone know what you mean, how you feel, or what you plan on doing.

If you tell your friend that you are going to go to his house to help him get to the next level with his video game, but you spend the entire night watching TV instead, what do you think that your friend is going to think? Yes, mistakes happen, and yes, sometimes you will have the best intentions of keeping your word to someone and still find that you're not able to do it. However, if the same "mistake" keeps happening, then people won't see it as just a "mistake" for long.

Try to guess the next number:

1,3,5,7,9,___

If you guessed "11", you have discovered the correct pattern. A pattern helps you to make a good guess of what the next number will be in the set, or in our example, what the next thing that you will do based on what you've done before in the past. If you keep making promises to your friend or family member that you will do something, but you keep "not keeping" your word, then that person will figure out your pattern soon enough. Next time he/she wants help with their video game or project, or wants to ask you to play at their house, or wants to invite you to the movies, they will most likely remember your pattern from the past. That is why it is important to make sure that your actions and your words match up with each other. If you say that you want one thing, but you keep doing something else instead, then people will soon realize that

you are not really a person of your word, and they won't know which to believe, your actions or your words.

1. If you say that you want to earn money by doing extra chores, but you complain to your parents about having to do work, will your parents think you want to earn extra money?

2. If you promise your parents that you will do your best in math class, but you keep leaving your math book in your school desk (making it impossible to do your math homework), will your parents think you are doing your best?

3. If you tell your friend Katy that you like her a lot, but you tell someone else that Katy is a jerk who doesn't know how to do anything, will anyone believe that you really like Katy?

When your words match your actions, you have some integrity. The definition of integrity is "strict personal honesty" (yes, from the same dictionary). People will feel they can trust you only when you've shown them integrity. Regardless of whether others see or sense your integrity, have it for yourself. If you don't have integrity with yourself, how do you expect anyone else to see it or sense it in you?

7.

Bad things sometime happen to good people.

YOU:

A good child that would make any parent proud. You are respectful of other people's feelings and belongings. You do your best at your most important job: SCHOOL. Your friends enjoy being around you, and they seem to ask to play with you often. You help your parents and you do your part in order to contribute to try to help make the household run smoothly. You don't do any of the things that Santa Claus warns you not to do (shout, pout or cry in order to get your way). Yep, you're a good child.

YOUR DAY:

Your day starts off like any other. You shower, get dressed for school, eat your breakfast, take a little time to watch tv or play a game, and you're off to school. You get on the school bus and walk to find a seat. You sit beside your best friend each day, but you don't see him today. There is only one seat left on the bus, and it's beside someone that you don't know at all. It turns out to be a new kid at school- Christine. Christine is very tall, and in fact, is much taller than anyone else on the bus. You sit next to her while still wondering where your friend is and why he had to be sick this day of all days (leaving you to sit beside this gigantic ogre of a girl). All of a sudden, the bus driver makes a sudden turn and the next thing you know, you are sitting in the lap of the gigantic beast Christine! Arrrgggghhhh! But that's not the worst part... your next best friends Brendan and Zach have seen you in the lap of this GIRL and are pointing at you and laughing while telling everyone that the two of you are boyfriend and girlfriend! EEE GAD!

You know what's coming next.... "{insert your name here} and CHRISTINE sitting in a tree, K-I-S-S-I-N-G, first comes love, second comes marriage..."

Your life is ruined right? You'll never be able to show your face at the lunch table again, right? You may as well drop out of school right now and hide from everyone and work at your paper route for the rest of your life, right? Wrong. Though this may have been embarrassing for you (and possibly for Christine too), it is not the end of life as you know it. Things are going to happen. You may trip on your shoelace in front of your friends, you may leave the lunchroom with ketchup on your nose without knowing it, or you may spill water on your pants in a spot that makes you look like you've had an accident. You may feel that these are bad things, and may not understand why they are happening to you. We've all had something on the tip of our noses; we've all tripped while someone saw us; and we've all been embarrassed by something that someone has done or said to us or about us. Ask your parent to share with you some examples from their lives.

Not only is tomorrow another day, but 3 o'clock is another hour.

8.

When bad things happen, it doesn't mean it's a totally bad DAY.

So many things happen to you during all of the hours of one day. You talk to people, listen to what people say to you, do things, and watch things being done. You will call some of the things that are said and done "good", but some are not going to seem so good.

★ Someone you thought was your friend might say something to you that you think is mean.

★ Your teacher may surprise your class with a math quiz.

★ You might walk right into your sparring partner's glove at karate.

★ You might forget your project on the dining room table.

★ You might trip on your shoelace on your way to school and in front of the entire school bus full of kids (and they might laugh).

★ You may have misplaced one of your favorite Pokemon action figures.

If all of these things were to happen all in one day, you would have a good case for calling the day a bad one. Usually, however, just one or two "bad" things happen in a day. A strange thing happens when one or two "bad" things happen to us. We tend to forget all of the good things that happen that day, and only seem to remember or want to talk about the bad thing. To top it all off, we will call the whole day bad just because of the one or two bad things that happened.

Here's a test. Take or imagine a piece of paper and divide it into 20 equal parts. Now, take or imagine that you have a green crayon and color in 18 of those squares green. Now, take or imagine that you have a red crayon, and color in the last 2 squares red. Would you call the paper mostly red? Of course not. But that is exactly what we do when we call the whole day bad just because of a few red squares. Can you still see that piece of paper in your mind? Those 18 squares CLEARLY mean that the paper is mostly green. Even if there were 6 good things and 2 bad things, your day can still be a good one.

For those days that seem really bad…the days where there are 6 bad things and only 2 good ones, just remember the saying "this too shall pass". Also remember that when things seem bad, they could always be worse.

We were given 2 ears and only one mouth for a reason.

Look at your face in the mirror. You have eyes, ears, a nose and a mouth. Now take a look and notice that you have 2 ears and only one mouth. Just for the sake of being clear, let's go over what each part is for:

Ears- for hearing, listening, taking in

Mouth- for speaking, talking

So now, back to our face count. Two ears: that means that you have double the power and double the ability of hearing and listening to whoever is talking to you (parents, friends, others). One mouth: you have one "machine" that can be used for getting your message across to everyone else. You have twice as much of an ability to listen as you do to speak.

What does all of this mean? People like to be listened to (and actually, you belong to this same group of people). So lucky for you that almost everyone that you meet and become friends with have two devices that they can use to hear what you say and hopefully listen to you. (By the way, "hear" and "listen to you" don't mean that they will do as you say or even like what you say). You need to try to return the favor for the people in your life. Do the same thing for them that you like to be done for you. Use your two ears to really listen to what the people around you are trying to say to you.

That doesn't mean that you have to listen to everything that people say to you (unless it's your parent/guardian), especially if you are sure that the person means to hurt you. Sometimes, people may be saying hurtful things to you for reasons that you won't be sure of or even understand. When this happens, imagine that their words are written down on a piece of paper, and make that paper into the shape of a paper airplane (or anything that flies). Imagine that the airplane is headed toward one of your ears. You have 3 choices when the plane is headed towards your ear:

Put your hand up and block the plane from getting in.

Duck your head so that the plane won't reach you.

Let the plane enter.

Even if the plane enters your ear, you still have another choice. You can let the plane with that load of words stay inside your head, or you can do something different. You can force that plane of words out of your head, make it come out the other ear, and then grab that plane in your hands, crumble it up and throw it onto the ground into a ball of fire. The choice is yours.

Unless a person is hurting you with their words, try your best ☺ to listen to what is being said to you.

10.

What you REALLY believe is true or will happen, probably will.

Suppose you get invited to a skating party. A lot of your friends are going to be there, and for that reason, you are looking forward to going. There's one problem though. You've only skated two times before in your whole life. As the date for the party gets closer and closer, you start to panic a little because you are afraid that you're going to fall down and that your friends are going to laugh at you. In fact, you begin to get so scared that you tell your parents that you don't want to go. Your parents tell you that everything will be fine and not to worry. They also say that it is too late to cancel because they already told the mom and dad of the birthday kid that you'd be there. You will have two choices as you make your way into the roller rink. You can either decide to give it your best shot and know that you'll have a good time no matter what happens, or you can continue to think that it's going to be the most embarrassing and awful time of your life. Either way, you will probably be right. What you believe will happen, can happen, and probably will happen.

If you believe something will be awful, you'll be preparing for it. You'll be thinking about it, and you may even be looking for it. When you look hard enough for something, it's a very good possibility that you will find it. So if it's a bad time that you're expecting and looking for, you'll find examples of it around you. On the other hand, if you tell yourself that you'll have a good time, you'll see good times all around you. Seeing those good times may make you smile, and then help you to have a good time. See how it works?

It has been said that each day, you will have close to 60,000 thoughts going through your mind. If most of those thoughts are about you failing,

messing up, or being in any way less than great, then you probably will be. By the same token, if you use most of your 60,000 thoughts thinking of you being successful or good at what you do or try, then you most likely will be. By the way, this doesn't really work that well with having thoughts of a toy or a gift appearing like magic under your pillow as you sleep. Nice try though!

Next time you walk or drive past some cars, see if you can find any that say FORD on the back of them. The man who was responsible for building one of the greatest auto companies (Ford Motor Company) was Henry Ford. One of the things that he liked to say was: "If you think you can, you can. And if you think you can't, you're right".

Enough said.

Every problem doesn't belong to you.

When a problem comes knocking on your front door, you may not know what to do with it. Just imagine that you are sitting on the living room sofa, the doorbell rings, and your mom answers the door. She walks up to you and says "It's for you." You get up, walk to the door, and open it. You see a large box with arms, legs and a head sticking out of it. When you look closer, you see that there is a giant label on the box that has your name on it written in large black letters. It looks like it's for you, and it's waving its hands like it is waving "hello" to you. Only problem is, you don't know whether it's safe to let it in, and now that you're thinking about it, you can't even think of where you're going to put it because your mom and dad just finished telling you that your room has too much stuff in it already.

What do you do with this problem? First, you make absolutely sure that the problem really does belong to you. Just because a problem might get delivered to your doorstep in a nice package with fancy colors and bows on it does not mean that it was meant for you to have. You must check to make sure that there isn't another label on it that tells who the real owner is of the package or problem. Once you're sure that the problem is yours, that doesn't mean that you have to bring it into your house, cook dinner for it and make it feel warm and cozy in your house.

Bringing problems into your home is a lot like bringing a stray cat into your home. Even cute, furry and fluffy stray cats can sometimes bring surprises to your home that you may not be ready to handle. Imagine if that cute, furry and cuddly cat was going to have eight baby kittens (true story that happened to one of my friends)? What she thought was only going to be one cat turned into one cat and eight kittens. Some people would enjoy having cute cuddly fur balls in their home, and you might be one of those people. However, problems are rarely that cute and cuddly.

So what do you do with the problem? You can figure out what to do with it if the problem isn't a quiet one and you need to deal with it right away in order to make it go away. You could also leave it outside on the doormat if you don't have to make a decision right now. Sometimes, if you wait, an answer to your problem may become clearer and appear after you've had time to think about it. If you're having a hard time trying to figure out how to solve a problem, don't be afraid to ask for help from people that you trust. You could ask your parent, guardian, brother or sister, friend, teacher, cub scout leader, or anyone else that you trust. Remember, that's why they were given two ears... the better to hear you with!

Try not to say "always" or "never".

Nothing is ALWAYS one way or another way. Even when it seems that something is always one way, it rarely is. For some reason, people like to use the word "always":

"You always get to go first when we're playing a game."

"I always have bad days at school."

YOU ALWAYS TALK MEAN TO ME.

Same thing with the word NEVER:

"You never let me have my way."

"I never get the chance to go first."

"I never get to eat the snack that I want to eat."

When you use words like ALWAYS and NEVER, you are really saying that things are always the same, or that they never change. We're going to talk about how things change all the time all around us, in the next section. When you use the word ALWAYS or NEVER, you are probably using it because you feel like something unfair has happened, or that you want something to change. When was the last time that you used the word ALWAYS or NEVER? Do you remember what you said? When you think about what you said, do you think that what you were really trying to say is that you want something to change or that you think something was unfair?

The next time you want to use the word ALWAYS or NEVER to someone, think about this: what is it that you REALLY want to have happen? Do you want to eat a certain snack? Go first when you play a game? Want the person to talk nicer to you? Want to have your opinion listened to and taken into consideration sometimes? Try saying that to the person that you're talking to. Here's why. The minute you use the word ALWAYS or NEVER to someone, you will immediately activate something in them. Think of it as little helpers that are inside that person's mind that will be running around searching the files and memories to find all the times that they DID do what you told them that they NEVER did. So if you tell your parent that you NEVER get to eat the snack that you want to eat, they will send their little helpers through their brain on a mission to find and remember all the times that they DID let you eat the snack that you wanted to eat. Then, they'll tell you that first of all, you were wrong, and second, they will list all the times that you asked for and ate doughnuts, candy and Popsicles. Once they do that, they will be concentrating on how they were right, and you were wrong. That's not what you wanted, right? All you really wanted was to be able to get the snack that you wanted today, or to go first in the game that you're playing right now. So if that's what you really wanted then say that. Then, you can give the little helpers a chance for them to get the snack that they really want!

13.

The only thing that is constant is change. (the only thing that will stay the same is that things will change)

The world all around you is changing. People are growing and getting older, and even the way your city looks is changing every year. You may have said for the past 3 years that purple was your favorite color but now say that it's blue. You couldn't wait to get a Star Wars GameBoy cartridge for Christmas and played with it every day for three months because it was your favorite game, and now you may play a different game every day because IT is your new favorite. Some things may be your favorite things for the rest of your life. Ever since I was a young girl, my absolute favorite pizza was from a place called Vennari's. Now that I'm 39 years old, Vennari's pizza still gets my vote as being the best. That hasn't changed. But the people that I thought were my best friends in the whole world back when I was 9, 10 and even 11 years old…they were replaced by new best friends that I had when I was 12, 13, 14, and 15 years old. There have been people that have stayed my friends since the day I met them, but there are some that I'm sure are happily the best friend with some other lucky person.

When change happens in your life, it can feel scary. When you're used to doing things one special way for a while, you get used to it and begin to think that it's always going to be that way (oops, there's that word ALWAYS…remember?). You wake up each day in the same house and say to yourself, "Okay, I know that my parents are downstairs, we're going to eat something that I've had before, my cat is going to purr when I rub him, and I'm going to see my best friend Ethan today in school." Every one of those things could change (hopefully not all at once).

What if:

★ Your parents sold the house and the family was moving to another one?

★ One of your parents had to work in another state for the next 6 months?

★ One of your parents decides that your favorite sausage biscuit is not good to have for breakfast anymore?

★ Your cat starts and keeps biting anyone who touches him?

★ Your best friend moves three states away?

In life, these are all examples of things that can happen. Things can be one way on Friday and be completely different on Monday. When those changes happen, you can either complain about them every day and stay in your room to protest the change in the hopes that it will change back (doubtful that this will work), or you can accept that change is something that we all have to face and try your best (remember about your best?) to keep up with those changes and not let them stop you from growing, learning and claiming the special life that is being created JUST FOR YOU. Feel free to take some time to get used to the change and to decide how you can turn it into something that benefits or helps you, but don't let the change stop you in your tracks for too long. Ask your parents and friends around you for help in this area, if you need it. You might just find out that something even better is waiting for you just around the corner.

14.

You may not understand why your parents did X, but you have to respect it (and them).

The X in this sentence could be anything:

Your parents could decide when you're in the 4th grade that your bedtime is 9pm, but change your bedtime to 8:30pm in the 5th grade. Now that won't make much sense to you, because you'll think "Hey, I'm older now, so shouldn't that mean that my bedtime gets pushed back?"

Your parents may tell you that you are absolutely not allowed to go to the nearby lake and park without telling them and without an adult who they know. Yet, you see other kids there having fun, laughing and playing and don't understand why you can't be with them too. You may say "It only takes 3 minutes to walk there from our house…and besides, aren't you always telling me to meet new people?"

Or your parents may have bought 3 doughnuts from the store and they are now at home preparing dinner for the family. You're starving, and you ask if you can have a snack before dinner. Your parents, knowing that dinner won't be ready for another 45 minutes, tell you that you can. You reach for the doughnut bag, hoping to polish off all 3 doughnuts, (because that's just how hungry you are) but your mom tells you that you can only have one.

Unless your parents are being abusive to you in some way, the things that they do and say to you are meant to help you, not hurt you. Your parents are most likely doing their best (there's that word again) to raise you in a way that will help ensure that you have a healthy and happy life. It's easy to look at someone else's life and wonder why you can't do things the way that they seem to be able to do them. It's also easy to

assume (another one of our words from earlier) that your parents are trying to hurt you, bother you, keep you from something fun, or that they just don't understand why it's so important that you be able to do X (remember, this could be anything)...that they're ruining your life.

Your parents have probably been on the face of the Earth at least 15 years longer than you. That's 15 years worth of happy times, sad times, bad times and "just okay" times. So, they've had a lot more experience than you at solving problems and making decisions (some good and some bad ones). The bottom line is that your parents are probably much better qualified (competent or capable) at figuring out what's the best for you, at least for now. They've earned that right because they've been here figuring things out a lot longer than you have. And frankly, it is their job to do it. Yes, parenting is a job that your parents or guardians have 24 hours a day, 7 days a week, 365 days a year. Your job is to go to school and learn as much as you can and do your best...but you only do that job maybe 5 days out of the week for 8 hours or so a day, with holidays and vacations. Well, imagine if you HAD to go to school or learn 24 hours a day, 7 days a week, 365 days a year? Could you handle that? Let your parents do their job and you do yours. Be glad that for now, most of those hard decisions that your parents have to make are being made by them and not you. The time will come soon enough when your parents will hand over the keys to the car of your life, and you'll get to drive where you want and when you want.

It won't kill you to thank your parents for their work (good or bad)

So now that you understand that your parents have one of the hardest and time-consuming jobs on the face of the earth (you'll realize this when it's your turn to be a parent), here's a hint on something that you can do to help your parents do their best (ah, see you weren't the only one who's supposed to do their best). Along with you doing your best at your job (school) and your family responsibilities, you can take time out every now and then and praise your parents for their efforts. (If you don't know what praise means, then it's your turn to find a dictionary and look it up...or look it up online...or ask one of your parents...and by the way, after they tell you, thank them for being so smart and for helping you). Your parents cook for you, give you field trip money, take you to practice, take care of you when you're sick, help you with homework, and many other things.

While it is true that it is your parent's job to raise you the best that they can, it is not their only responsibility in life. Your parents probably have a boss and customers that they have to answer to at work, there may be other kids (your brothers or sisters) that they have to take care of, they have to try to peacefully work together with your other parent or guardian to raise the kids, and they have to try to take care of themselves (sometimes with what little energy or money there is left over).

You know how you love it when your parent or your teacher tells you that you've done a good job doing something? Maybe you got a good report card, or maybe you earned a stripe on your karate belt, or maybe your teacher wrote "outstanding work" on the assignment that you turned in last week. Do you remember how you felt when you were told what a good job you've done? Didn't you smile inside (and maybe it showed outside too)? You felt like you were on top of the world, didn't you? You had a lot to be proud of yourself for... whatever you achieved or accomplished was great. But the words that you heard from someone who saw what you did and told you that you did good...those were just as powerful as your achievement. Even if you didn't do great, fabulous or even good at what you tried to do, don't you sometimes hear from a parent, teacher or friend that you still did good? These are the people that care about you the most. They are the people that want to cheer you up and who want to see you get back up after being knocked down. They don't want you to give up and not try again just because you didn't get an A on the test or that stripe on your belt (this time).

You care about your parents don't you? They care about you. Find some time to thank them every now and then for all that they do for you...even though you may not be able to see what they do and don't know all of the things that they do for you. Give to others what you wish and want them to give to you. Do it even though they may not ALWAYS give it back to you. Being nice to others doesn't guarantee that they will be nice to you. But you can feel good about the fact that you were nice, and you were being who you are. You get a reward no matter what the other person does or doesn't give you.

16.

Know when to back off.

If you're talking to your parents about the fact that your bedtime has changed, or that they want to limit your time in front of the television, you have the right to feel the way that you feel about the issue. You may have a family that encourages you to speak your mind and let your thoughts be known. If that is the case, good for you. Feel free to politely ask your parents or guardians why they decided to make the decision that they made. Ask them if you can tell them your thoughts on the matter. If they say yes, then go ahead and nicely but calmly tell them how you feel and why you feel it should be different than what they've decided. You may bring up reasons to them that they hadn't thought of before, and they may change their mind. However, you need to be prepared for the real possibility that they won't change their mind, and that what they said is how it's going to be. The wrong thing to do at this point would be to keep asking the same thing of your parents over and over again. Once they have already made a decision about something, and they tell you that they don't want to discuss it again, or they aren't going to change their mind, you would be doing yourself and your parents a favor by not trying to bring it up yet again.

The same thing applies to your friends, your teachers, and even people that you don't know so well. At some point, we all say "enough is enough". If we keep telling our friend that the girl that they like is totally wrong for them, at some point, they're not going to want to hear you say it anymore. When your friend reaches that point, he or she will most likely do one of three things:

1.   no longer call you their friend
2.   get mad at you for pestering them about something they like or decided

3. decide that you are right and forget about the girl

It's not likely that your parent will stop calling you their son or daughter, but it's also not likely that they will decide that you're right about the issue and change their mind (though it may happen). However, your parent could get upset that you are continuing to challenge their authority (and basically trying to do their job). If a parent or friend feels strongly about an issue and you don't agree, if you're able to say your thoughts to them, then do so, but do it ONCE (twice only if they ask you to). After that, they know how you feel, and there is no need to keep stuffing it down their throat. In the end, it could work against you.

"Opportunity is missed by most because it knocks on the door and is dressed like work."

The famous inventor Thomas Edison said that. What does it mean, you ask?

First, a definition of opportunity: "a favorable time or occasion for a certain purpose". Okay, you may still need more of an explanation here. Opportunity can also mean just a plain old chance to do something... usually something that you want. So onto Mr. Edison's saying.

Let's say that you are looking for ways to earn some extra money so that you can buy something special that you want. You've already asked your parents for the money, and they've turned you down flat. You're already doing some extra chores, but it doesn't seem to be giving you the extra money fast enough. You're on your way home from school, and you're playing in your mind some of the things that have happened at school.

A kid from the classroom next to yours got sent to the principal's office.

The burger at lunch tasted pretty good today.

You had fun with your friends out at recess.

You finished your homework during free time.

You learned about recycling paper, plastic and aluminum in class.

You're walking down the street and you notice that one of your neighbors is carrying a box of soda cans out to the curb. When you look closer, you see that there are 4 more boxes sitting on the front porch, waiting to be taken to the curb. As you walk toward your house, you notice

for the first time that almost all of the houses in your neighborhood have already put out at least a bag or a box of cans at the curb. You go into your house, shut the door, go up to your room, and dream of the day when you will be able to buy that special thing. After dinner, your mom reminds you that you have to take the recycling out to the curb (one of the ways you help your family and house). You take out a couple of bags of paper and cans to the curb. You walk back into the house and think once again of asking your parents for the money, but you decide not to do it because you remembered that they already told you what they thought about it. The next day on your way to school, you pass a green recycling truck and watch as the truck crunches up the plastic, paper and cans. Then you remember seeing the movie in class about the aluminum can place that paid people for their cans. You think that your neighbors should have seen the movie, and you walk to your class. Did you miss something? Rewind this story in your head: you see movie in school about recycling; you pass people in your neighborhood who recycle; you want money to be able to buy X (anything). Connect the dots.

Will it take some work to ask your neighbors if you can collect their cans, and then to ask your parents if you can keep them in the backyard? Yes. Is this an opportunity to get what you want? You bet! Opportunity, dressed up as work. What opportunities have you missed because you thought it looked too much like work and thought it wouldn't help you with anything that you wanted?

18.

Treat people how you would like to be treated.

You've probably heard this one before from one of your parents, a teacher, or someone in your family. If you have, read this again because it is one of the easiest ways that you can have power and control over your life.

I'll start with a story. While driving down the street with three 9 year old kids in the car, we passed by a man standing out in the cold who was holding a sign in his hand. One of them read the sign out loud: "Please help. Will work for food." One of the other kids said, "Wow, that guy is homeless. I'd give him about 2 cents." They all laughed and started talking about something else. I asked them a question:

"If it was you that was out on that corner, and you didn't have a job or any money, and you were holding out that sign and hoping that someone would read it and help you out, then how would you feel if some kids came by and said "I'd give him about 2 cents" and then laughed?"

It's not really important how these kids answered my question. What is important is how you would answer it. How would you feel if someone said that to you? And the next question for you is "What would you want people to do if you had no money, no food and had made a sign asking for help because you really needed it?"

Before you decide how you are going to talk to someone, or how you will treat them, you should first try to think about how you'd want them to treat or talk to you.

If you want people to be nice to you, be nice to others.

If you want people to help you, then help others.

If you want people to talk nice to you, then talk nice to others.

If you want people to listen to you, then listen to them.

In many instances, you will have a better chance of getting from others what you yourself give. If you are caring and understanding to a friend that needs it, you may find that there is a time when you will need (and will get) care and understanding. If you are helpful and giving to people who may need it, you may experience a time in your life when you need (and get) help from others. This doesn't mean that you will ALWAYS get help, caring and understanding if you give it. But if you want IT (whatever IT is), give it!

19.

Learn empathy and have empathy for others.

It's time for another definition. Empathy is "Identification with and understanding of another's situation, feelings and motives." This means that you try to put yourself in someone else's shoes.

If your friend's pet just died yesterday and tells you today that they don't want to go to your birthday party, don't be so quick to get upset with your friend for not coming to your party. Try to understand how they may be feeling about the loss of their pet. Would you want to be around other people after you lost your favorite pet?

Suppose you want to go to the toy store tonight after dinner to check out the latest toys. Now let's say your mom had to work from 9 in the morning until 7 at night and she walks into the house looking tired and talking about how tired she is. You remind her that she said she'd take you to the toy store, but your mom says "Sweetie, I am too tired to do anything except take off my shoes and sit down. We'll have to do that another day." You are kind of crushed, but can you see why your mom may be feeling the way she does? She was at work for 10 hours, and then had to drive home. I know that you may think that she can drive you to the store real quick, and that it won't take long at the store, but can you understand why SHE may not want to do it today? Have you ever been tired of walking, and didn't even want to think of walking with your parents through the mall while they went shopping? So then you know how it feels, right?

Sometimes, you should think about what the other person is going through BEFORE you tell them how you're feeling. Sometimes, the needs of others are going to be more important than your needs. Sometimes, your needs are going to be more important than those of others. You will need to learn to take turns, and don't hog it all up for yourself.

Why should you have empathy, you ask? Because remember, people like to think and feel that you care about them and want to hear what it is that they have to say. If you care about what others are feeling, experiencing and going through, then there is a greater chance that they will care about what you are feeling, experiencing or going through. Caring only about yourself, only about what you are going through, and only about what you want, is selfish. People do not like being around selfish people...at least not for long. When one person does all of the talking, and only talks about themselves, it quickly becomes a boring conversation. The very definition of CONVERSATION is "an informal spoken exchange." EXCHANGE means "to give and receive..." So, the only way that two people can have a conversation is if BOTH people are participating. If one of them does all the talking, it's not a conversation.

Care about what others are thinking, going through, and doing. Ask questions about what is going on in the lives of the people that you care about. That's one of the best ways that you can let them know that you care. Have empathy for them, and you'll increase the chances that they'll have empathy for you.

20.

Everyone has something to contribute to the world.

Look around you...all around you. Look at the people in the stores and in the mall, the kids at your school, the people who live in your grandma's city, the people who you pass when you're riding in the car, and any other living person that you see. Every person that you meet, and even those that you won't ever meet, they all have something to contribute to this world.

You may not understand what it is that a person has to contribute. You may meet someone and at first think that they couldn't possibly have anything to contribute to the world. You may meet one of the meanest bullies ever who smells bad and acts like they don't know anything about anything. If you think that person will never be anything special in life, you may be making a wrong assumption (remember about assumptions? If not, go back to page 21)

There is a saying that you may have heard before. If not, then pay close attention to this: Never judge a book by its' cover. You may not like the colors, the shapes or even the title on the cover of the book, but that doesn't mean that the book won't give you laughs, enjoyment, wisdom, or useful information. The same with people. You will meet people who look very different from you. You will meet people who have different ideas, hair, abilities, skin color, strengths, body size, weaknesses, and religions from you. Just because they are different, does not mean that they don't have something to offer or teach you. Some of your greatest teachers will be people that don't look, act or even sound like you. Think of some of the schoolteachers that you've had so far. How many of them had black hair? Blonde hair? Were women? Were men? Acted weird the first day you met them? How many did you think were mean at first?

How many taught you something? Have you ever watched someone do something on television, and then thought to yourself, "I'd like to try to do that because it looks like fun." If you tried it and liked it, you have that person to thank for it.

If you count someone that you meet as a waste of your time, or think that they are so different from you that they couldn't possibly have anything to offer you, you will sadly miss out on a lot in the world. Of course, you should also ask yourself the following question based on what has been written already in this book: Will you like it if people count you out as a waste of their time because you look different from them? Do you think that you don't have any value or anything to offer to others or to the world? So, are you treating others the way that you want them to treat you?

The bottom line is that we can learn something from everyone that we meet.

21.

Resist comparing yourself to others... appreciate your unique gifts/situation.

When you think of other people, you may think that they have more of something than you, can do something better than you, or have more chances than you. It is true that there will be people that you meet that will be able to do things that you can't do right now. And it is also true that there will be people that are better at a sport, schoolwork, or games than you. But it is also true that there are things that you can do very well, and even better than others can do.

You are unique in many ways. When you try to make a list of things that you are good at, the list may be a short one right now. As you get older and you experience more things in life, you will develop talents that you don't yet know that you have. As was mentioned in the last section, we all have something to contribute to the world. Even if you don't know what those things are yet, be patient. You'll become aware of them soon enough. If you think about it, you will probably be able to come up with something that you do very well. Ask your friends and family what they think you do very well. You may be surprised to hear how they will answer you.

Once you learn that there are things that you are good at, or are good about your life, appreciate yourself for having those gifts. A special talent or a unique situation can sometimes be thought of as a gift, and more importantly, you should think of them as gifts. Practice your skills, and make them even better. Guard them carefully, and protect them from laziness. Remember the saying "practice makes perfect?" Well, laziness makes loss. It has been reported that Michael Jordan practiced basketball almost every day of his life since he was a young teen. Talk about practice makes perfect! When people think of one of the great players in basketball, they think of Michael Jordan. The same for Larry Bird, Sheryl Swoopes and others who have developed their talents in sports, education, and in play.

If Michael Jordan had spent a lot of time comparing himself to other players, he wouldn't have had as much time to practice and perfect his skills. If you spend your time sitting around comparing yourself to others and talking about how you WISH you could be like Mr. Or Miss X, you may soon find that others are out making YOUR dream come true.

22.

The things that come to those that wait are the things left over by those who got there 1st.

Okay, now here's an assignment for you. Go to your parent or guardian, and ask them if they've ever heard of the following saying:

"Good things come to those that wait."

Almost everyone has heard of that saying. What it means is: Don't rush to make decisions and, if you don't, your patience may be rewarded in the future. If you are faced with two or even three choices for what to do, sometimes, the best thing to do is NOT DECIDE right now. If the decision has to be made by a certain time, then by all means, make a decision. However, if you're having a hard time deciding, time can sometimes work to help you. Sometimes, things become clearer as time goes on.

While there is certainly some value and good points to waiting for things that you really want, there is also some value to another saying: You snooze, you lose. If you have an opportunity in front of you to do something or to get something, and you are sleeping, will you be able to get it or do it? Most likely, the answer is NO. Same with most of life. If you wait to do something when you think that it will be safe, or when you think you are guaranteed to be successful at it, you will probably be waiting too long. If opportunity knocks at your door and you are waiting to answer (or even to decide to answer), opportunity may knock again, or it may decide that you're not interested and go knocking on someone else's door! Decide today that when opportunity knocks, you will at least come to the door and let it know that you're THINKING of letting it come in. If you don't, you can believe that someone else will.

While you have your parent or guardian nearby, ask them if they've heard of this saying: The early bird gets the worm. Let's imagine that there are five baby birds that are all hungry. Each one wakes up at a different time and starts looking for breakfast. If there is one worm and there are 5 hungry birds, which one will have the greatest chance of getting the worm? The one that woke up at 10 in the morning and started watching tv, or the one who woke up at 8 in the morning and went out hunting for food?

Decide today that when opportunity knocks, you will answer. Decide today that sometimes, YOU are going to be the early bird that gets the worm. And as always, check with your parent or guardian to be sure that what you think is a great opportunity is really truly a good one.

23.

You can choose to look at it differently (a cloudy day or are plants getting a break from sun?)

Know how you are sometimes happy when the weekends are here? A break from school, a break from homework, a break from whatever. Well, even the plants that are outside need those same sort of break at times. What do they need a break from, you ask? Almost every day, plants are being shined on by the sun. Some days, the heat from the sun is downright brutal, and beats down on those plants and grass like a heavy weight. Some plants really like all of that sunshine, but some would be fine with just a little of the sun. Imagine what would happen if the plants and grass got sunshine for three weeks straight, but didn't get any water. Plants and grass need so much more than just the sunlight in order to grow and stay healthy. They need sunlight, water and minerals like those found in the ground. While the sun is usually fantastic for the grass and plants, too much of something (even good things) isn't always good. The same goes for you. If you spent your entire life doing nothing but going to school, you might turn out to be extremely intelligent, but there is a lot that you would be missing out on in life. There is so much more to life than just school, just video games, or just having fun playing games.

In your life, you will find that there are things that you really enjoy, and then there will be things that you'd rather skip or do without. When you get comfortable doing the things that you really like to do, new things can seem like a drag and un-important. Your parents, guardians, and teachers will introduce some of those things to you. Remember, we said before that you won't always understand WHY your parents or guardians do things or make the decisions that they make, but you do have to respect them? Well, the same goes for doing activities that your parents MAKE you do or participate in. When those times come when your parents/ guardians make you try something out, do something, or participate in some activity that feels new and weird to you, just remember that you have a very powerful muscle that you can use anytime that you want. I'm not talking about the one on your arm; I mean the one that is in your head.

Every one of us only uses a small amount of the brainpower that we have at our disposal. We don't even use half of our total brainpower. There will never be any danger of you filling your brain up with so much information that your brain will fill up...that's just impossible to do. We each have the power in us to choose to think of things differently. You may feel yourself starting to feel one way about something, and just at that moment, you can choose to think something totally different about it. With our example about the plants and flowers: if it rains every day for 4 days, yes, you will think that it's yucky outside and you'll be anxious for it to stop raining. You can also think that the rainy day is somehow bad because it gets in the way of you getting to play outside at recess or at home, or you could choose to look at it another way. You could think of it as the plants and grass are getting the chance to stock up on water, and that they are getting a break from that hot, brutal sun. Your choice. If you let the rain outside spray your mood with cold, damp water, then it may as well be raining inside too.

24.

The Case of the Disappearing, Failing Grade.

Imagine that your friend Andrew gets a failing grade on every one of his math tests. He does good on his math homework, but you notice that all of his tests so far have had D's written on them when the teacher hands them back. You can't understand why he gets A's on his homework and D's on his test, so you ask him. He tells you that he can't understand it either, and that his parents are pretty upset about it. He says that he wants to get good grades on his tests, but that he doesn't know how. Being the friend that you are, you decide to help him figure out and solve the mystery. You ask him a bunch of questions:

Are you studying at home for the test?

Did you get good sleep the night before the test?

Do you understand the materials? (You must since you get As on your homework)

Did you have enough time to finish the test?

Andrew answers "yes" to every question, so it becomes even more of a mystery to both of you. Your friend says "I'm really upset, because the test grade is making my class grade go down, and my parents don't think that I'm studying because of the grade I'm getting on the tests." You both decide to look at one of his tests to see what happened.

Problem #1: $10 + 5 + 2$

Andrew's answer on the test is "7". When you read the problem to Andrew, he says, "Yeah, the answer is 17." You show the test to Andrew and point to the answer that he wrote on the paper. Andrew says, "oh, I guess I made a mistake."

Problem #4: 15 – 5

Andrew's answer on the test is 20. Again, you read the problem to Andrew, and he gives the right answer to you, but he has written the wrong answer down on the test. You and Andrew find 5 more problems where Andrew has made a similar mistake. Your detective work has paid off! Andrew has not been reading the math problems correctly. He tells you that because he feels that the math is so easy for him, he hurries to get it done so that he can have some free time to doodle figures on his notebook cover.

Here's where you get to show that you are a caring friend. You tell Andrew that he should check over his work before he turns it in. You tell him that you have to carefully read the questions so that you are sure how you are supposed to answer them. You get to be a good friend by telling him that he really is smart, and that he will be able to prove it to everyone if he is more patient and careful with his work.

On his next test, he gets an A. Andrew is happy, his teacher is happy, his parents are happy, and you are happy that you could help. If you're going to get a math problem wrong, let it be wrong because you don't know the answer, not because you weren't paying attention to the questions.

25.

If you want something different, do something different.

★ If you fail tests because you don't study, try studying

★ If you don't make new friends because you don't talk to people, try talking to people.

★ If you want your parents to stop asking you to clean your room, clean it before they ask.

★ If you keep doing the same things, you will keep getting the same results.

No matter how hard you try, 2 + 2 will always equal 4. You start with 2, you add another 2, and you will get 4 - ALWAYS. If you earn $5 for washing Mr. Smith's car, and earn another $5 for washing Mrs. Johnson's car, you will have $10 at the end of the day (unless you spend some of it). If you want more money than $10, what will you have to do? You guessed it! Wash more cars or do something else to earn more money. The same goes for most of your life. If you want to have something different on the other end of that equal sign, you will have to do something different to the first side. Do something different to get something different.

Look at yourself in the mirror. All that you are... your strengths, your weaknesses, your knowledge, your skills, your feelings, everything that you have... is all the way on the left side of this equation in the "you now" space:

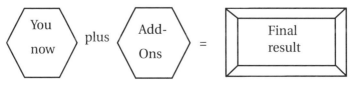

In the "add-ons" space, you have all of the things that you do in your life: talk to people, walk, learn something new, listen to people, read things, watch things, help people, do work, etc. And the "final result" is what happens when you add them both together. So, take the you that you are today, and add to that your actions and decisions. If you keep doing the same thing, you will get the same final result. Change you, or change what you do or what you say, and you'll likely get a different result.

If you point to someone else, remember, there are 3 fingers pointing back to you.

One of the favorite words that kids of all ages and of all times seem to enjoy saying and using is the word "stupid". The second definition of the word "stupid" in my trusty dictionary is "showing a lack of intelligence." How many times have you heard someone say:

1. "My stupid teacher gave us homework." (hum, teacher, stupid? Doesn't sound like it belongs in the same sentence according to our definition above).

2. "I can't believe that you said that. You're so stupid sometimes."

3. "That's the most stupid thing that I've ever heard."

Calling someone stupid or any other name is not nice. I hope that this has never happened to you, but how would you feel if someone called you stupid? If you call someone a name that isn't nice, it is just like you pointing a finger at that person. Imagine that you are pointing at someone. Go ahead, point to something in your room. Now, look down at your hand. You have that one finger that is pointing at whatever you are pointing to, and maybe your thumb is pointing in that direction too. Take a look at your other fingers. You have your middle finger, your ring finger and the pinky finger all pointing at guess who? YOU! So, you have maybe two fingers pointing at something or someone else, but three are pointing back at you. You should always remember that.

Before you say something about someone else, you should think about what it says about you. That's right, what it says ABOUT YOU. We all have our faults. None of us are perfect. Before you say anything

about the faults that you think that you see in someone else (whether you know the person or not), make sure that there isn't some fault about you that someone could also talk about. Most likely, there is some fault or imperfection about you that makes you just as human as the rest of us. Remembering that you should "do unto others as you would like them to do unto you", do you really want people to start calling you names or telling others about the things that you don't do 100% correctly?

Hold your hand up in front of you. Point to anything in the room. Now, while still pointing, turn your hand upside down so that you can see the palm of your hand. How many fingers are pointing back at you? Always remember this.

THE END.

Books I Recommend:

Don't Sweat the Small Stuff for Teens. By Richard Carlson, Ph.D. Hyperion, New York. 2000

Stay Strong: Simple Life Lessons for Teens. By Terrie Williams. Scholastic Inc., New York. 2001

The Teenager's Guide to the Real World. By Marshall Brain. BYG Publishing, Inc., Raleigh, NC 1997

Life Strategies For Teens. By Jay McGraw. Fireside, New York. 2000

Teens Can Make It Happen: Nine Steps to Success. By Stedman Graham. Simon & Schuster, New York. 2000

The Four Agreements: A Toltec Wisdom Book. By Don Miguel Ruiz. Amber-Allen Publishing, San Rafael, California. 1997

Think and Grow Rich: A Black Choice. By Dennis Kimbro and Napoleon Hill. Ballantine Books, New York. 1991

ORDER FORM

Fax or send your order to:
Inspired by the Beach Publishing
P.O. Box 174
Simpsonville, MD 21150-0174
Fax: 240-782-4222 • Phone: 877-411-TIME

SHIP TO:

_____   _____
Name   Company

_____
Street Address

_____   _____   _____
City   State   Zip

_____   _____
Telephone   email

BILL TO (If different from SHIP TO):

_____ Attn: _____
Company/School

_____
Street Address

_____   _____   _____
City   State   Zip

_____
Telephone

PAYMENT OPTIONS:
❒ Purchase order Attached: #_____
❒ Check enclosed (**make payable to _Inspired by the Beach Publishing_**)
❒ Paypal payment (**send payment to _info@corridorconcierge.com_**)

Quantity	Unit price	Total
	10.95	
Shipping	Add 10% Minimum $4.00	
	TOTAL